100 IDEAS
FOR SUPPORTING PUPILS WITH SOCIAL, EMOTIONAL AND BEHAVIOURAL DIFFICULTIES

ALSO AVAILABLE FROM CONTINUUM

100 IDEAS
FOR SUPPORTING PUPILS WITH SOCIAL, EMOTIONAL AND BEHAVIOURAL DIFFICULTIES

Roy Howarth

continuum

KH

This book is dedicated to Pam Fisher

Acknowledgements

With thanks to Emma Howarth, Andrew Lysley and Mary Fallows.

Continuum International Publishing Group

The Tower Building   80 Maiden Lane
11 York Road   Suite 704
SE1 7NX   New York, NY 10038

www.continuumbooks.com

© Roy Howarth 2008

British Library Cataloguing-in-Publication Data

A catalogue record for this book is available from the British Library.

ISBN: 08264 9661 (paperback)

Library of Congress Cataloging-in-Publication Data

Howarth, Roy.
    100 ideas for supporting pupils with social, emotional and behavioural difficulties / Roy Howarth.
        p. cm.
    ISBN-13: 978-0-8264-9661-4 (pbk.)
    ISBN-10: 0-8264-9661-X (pbk.)
    1. Problem children—Education. 2. Classroom management. 3. Behavior modification. I. Title. II. Title: Hundred ideas for supporting pupils with social, emotional and behavioural difficulties.

    LC4801.H65 2007
    371.94—dc22

Designed and typeset by Ben Cracknell Studios
www.benstudios.co.uk

Printed and bound in Great Britain by MPG Books Ltd, Bodmin, Cornwall.

8/28/09

CONTENTS

SECTION 3 The lesson

SECTION 4 Basic skills

SECTION 5 School documentation and support

SECTION 6 Measuring SEBD

SECTION 7 **Help from outside**

SECTION 8 **Communicating with pupils and parents**

SECTION 9 **Challenging behaviour and triggers**

SECTION 10 **Pre-empting escalation**

SECTION 11 Behaviour likely to escalate

SECTION 12 Interventions following escalation

SECTION 13 Crisis time

INTRODUCTION

Teaching. Do you love it? Do you hate it? Does its complexity drive you mad or is it simplicity itself? Are your pupils unteachable or are they little angels? Are you proud of your work or exhausted and demoralized? The chances are that at any point in your teaching career you will experience most of these conflicting emotions.

Teaching demands from its practitioners a stunning repertoire of skills: curriculum delivery, psychology and counselling, understanding and managing special educational needs, team membership/management, and coping with never-ending administrative tasks. Then there are the pupils with social, emotional and behavioural difficulties (SEBD) to manage.

But take courage! The strategies in this book have been tried and tested over many years with SEBD pupils, otherwise known as 'Sensationally Extremely Bloody Difficult, Significantly Every Bloody Day!' So, give the strategies a fair chance but, most of all, enjoy your work. SEBD pupils are intellectually challenging, even physically demanding. They are never easy to work with but they are very rewarding when you get it right.

SEBD pupils are labelled with different names, syndromes and acronyms. Their behaviours are attributed to many reasons, causes and consequences. However, when they walk into your classroom, they challenge you with the most difficult, demanding and often outrageous behavioural problems – the labels evaporate and solutions need to be found.

This book is here to be dipped into and used depending on what works best for you. We can't all be star teachers but we can become good enough at our job to progress with purpose and resolve. Being confident and positive about the future is good for our mental health and excellent for the pupils' well-being and learning abilities. After all, that is what the job is about . . . but do remember, too, that when there is friction between teacher and pupil, it is not always the pupil's fault. As teachers we need to look at ourselves and the quality of our interaction with our pupils.

Finally, there are no panaceas for managing SEBD pupils. You must be prepared to work hard, concentrate and, most of all, be rigorous and consistent about your teaching practice. SEBD pupils will not lie down and say, 'Thank you Sir/Miss.' The majority of them will not lose their hunger to destroy you, but will agree to 'get along and play the game' if you play it fair. Don't forget that just keeping them in the classroom and giving them an interest in learning are major achievements in their own right and not to be undervalued.

Depending on area and type of school the ratio of boys to girls with the more profound forms of SEBD tends to be around five to one. For simplicity, therefore, the child will be referred to throughout the book as 'him' or 'he'.

Looking at you

From the moment you get to school to the moment you leave through the school gates, you are a teacher. That is a role you have to play and modify to be successful. Your personality outside school can take on whatever form or shape you choose, but at school you are a teacher.

How you present yourself at school is the 'you' as seen by your pupils. Look at yourself in the mirror just before you go to school and ask yourself two basic questions:

○ How do the children see me?
○ How do I want the children to see me?

What do you think? Are you happy with your appearance? Do you look strong and interesting? Do you look confident?

How you dress is important too. Do you look tidy? Are you smart enough or too smart? Do you dress in keeping with your colleagues? Remember that what you choose to wear at school affects how you are perceived by all pupils, especially by SEBD pupils.

○ After a bad day at school, look again in the mirror and ask yourself what went wrong. Why did I do that? What did I say that for? Why was I like that? Was anything successful?
○ After a good day at school, look again in the mirror and ask why it all seemed so good today. What went right? Why did it click? Remember, it was *you* that got it right, no one else!

Many of these difficult children experience confused and contradictory parenting, particularly by way of personal care and the setting of boundaries. In the classroom you are the managing, caring adult whose job is to provide a safe, fair and predictable environment.

Teachers who are nervous and unsure about their ability to manage can sometimes respond too quickly and overreact to minor behavioural problems. This inflames the situation. Teachers also develop anxieties regarding their ability to manage difficult pupils. They will intervene the first time the child makes a wrong move, rather than wait for the right moment and then intervene decisively.

You need to:

○ start the lesson with a positive remark to the problem pupil. If possible, welcome him at the classroom door with a smile
○ deal non-verbally with minor misdemeanors
○ always start any intervention as slowly and quietly as the situation permits
○ rehearse internally what you are going to say when things get difficult
○ stay calm and don't jump into top gear as soon as trouble starts
○ refrain from disciplining from a distance or from such close range that the pupil feels threatened
○ take a deep breath and count to five!

DEFUSING SKILLS

Inexperienced teachers may lack defusing skills and, consequently, problems can escalate. SEBD children constantly challenge authority. They push and provoke in many different ways – standing up, bullying a neighbour, shouting, making silly or obscene remarks. In doing this, they are trying to catch your eye to see how you and the class will react. So, what can you do about this?

○ Always teach close to the difficult pupil, displaying concern and interest.
○ Present yourself as confident and in control (even if inside you feel like a jelly!).
○ Give a running commentary on what the pupil is doing, interjected with quiet responses.
○ Move closer but don't comment if things start to get difficult, just move closer still to the point where you are almost standing on the pupil's toes. If you do this without saying a word, the disturbance will often subside.
○ Stop the whole class from working and then ask the child to explain to the class something he has just learned and which he understands well.

The examples above are not direct challenges to difficult children but instead draw and shape the boundaries around them.

After each session write some brief notes identifying what worked for you and what didn't. Above all, don't repeat your mistakes.

Some teachers believe confrontation is the best way to resolve problems caused by difficult pupils. They tend to confront children, leaving them with few options to extricate themselves. This strategy is dangerous and can quickly lead to physical confrontation.

Examples of confrontational control are statements such as:

○ Stand behind your chair with your arms folded.
○ Take that gum out of your mouth.
○ Give me that mobile phone now.
○ Get out of my class immediately.

All these statements (and many more like them) may work with your average pupil but they are a red rag to our friends with SEBD. By making such remarks, you directly challenge the pupil in front of an expectant audience, leaving no avenue for escape.

Ask yourself the following questions. Why do you want him to stand behind his chair? Are you trying to achieve immediate obedience or just humiliation? Or do you want the offending behaviour to stop and the class to return to their work without interruption?

Instead, stop the whole class from working by asking everyone to stand up and then sit down again quietly.

Why do you want him to take the gum out of his mouth? What is more important here? Getting the gum removed immediately or maintaining class stability and teacher respect? Prioritizing the interests of the whole class is always the best strategy.

So, speak quietly to the gum-chewer and suggest that next lesson it might be better not to chew gum in class.

NOT BEING FAIR

Perhaps the greatest source of difficult behaviour results from inconsistent classroom management, or 'not being fair'. Difficult pupils can smell injustice from miles away. As a teacher, you must be scrupulously consistent in rewarding, praising, and correcting. Missing the chance to praise a difficult pupil will seem like deprivation to him, almost a denial of effort.

Typically, difficult pupils get labelled a lot by staff and other pupils. Every time they transgress the finger of accusation is pointed and the label is reinforced. Even when they are just one of a group of children 'in trouble', they are the ones singled out for specific blame. If you are called the devil often enough, you may as well be the devil!

When the children get things right, some teachers are so prejudiced in their hostility that they find it difficult to praise. So, in the end, in the minds of many SEBD pupils, the classroom becomes associated with injustice.

Try to create a classroom which is both fair and transparent, where difficult behaviour is managed consistently using clear guidelines that everyone understands and that are evenly applied. Be clear in your judgements, both positive and negative. Whenever possible, be positive in your comments because SEBD pupils rarely feel the warm rays of the sun at school!

The greatest escape route for some teachers is to be subjective about a child's difficulties. A child can be described as 'too difficult', 'too violent' or 'too mentally sick' to manage. He 'does not like me and hates my subject'. Although this may be true, the problem might equally be due to a teacher's lack of skills, empathy and experience. The bottom line is that unless a pupil is excluded, he will be back the next day!

Teachers who are persecuted by difficult pupils often respond by making very basic errors, which compound the problem. Here are a few classic errors that persecuted teachers make:

○ Excessive and/or continuous shouting at an individual child and/or class.
○ Persistently negative responses targeted at individuals and/or groups.
○ Talking about an individual's problems and behaviour in front of them and the class.
○ Humiliating children in front of their peers.

But what can you do to rectify this negative spiral?

○ Observe other teachers managing the same difficult pupils successfully.
○ Talk to other professionals about different tactics that might be tried.
○ Ask the senior management team (SMT) and the special educational needs coordinator (SENCO) for a meeting with the child and possibly the parent. It is advisable in this case to have notes of incidents that have occurred in the classroom.

In conclusion, it might be the teacher, it might be the subject, it might be the child that is too maladjusted to cope with school, but by searching for an answer you are on the way to solving the problem.

BEING SUBJECTIVE

ORAL COMMUNICATION

Oral communication is the sharpest tool you have in your teaching bag. Used well, it will help you manage both the class and the difficult pupil. Always choose your words carefully and speak clearly. Keep the language of management straightforward. These children are not always rewarded by listening to adults, so when addressing them and the whole class, keep it simple and unambiguous.

Vary the rate at which you speak. Use pauses and silences effectively. Vary the pitch, tempo and volume of your voice. Keep our special pupils on their toes. Make sure the structure of what you are saying is easy to follow. Don't speak over the heads of these reluctant learners otherwise they will switch off; their inadequacies and their low academic self-image will quickly bubble to the surface and that's when the trouble begins.

Speak pleasantly and use humour, keeping the volume of your voice as low as possible, leaving plenty in reserve. If you manage the class and individual pupils with a quiet voice, your classroom will feel like a calm and safe place.

Look for every opportunity to be positive, praising them with a smile. Search for good attitudes that you can reward. Develop some catch phrases that suit your personality and create class jokes about good behaviour – even use a funny voice if you feel confident enough to do so.

Use anger sparingly and with control and good timing. Practise your 'angry voice' in front of a mirror before you try it out at school. If you get anger 'wrong', you will make a fool of yourself and trouble will follow. These children love seeing teachers lose their temper and make fools of themselves.

What on earth have a teacher's writing skills got to do with controlling very difficult behaviour? Not a lot at first glance, but you might actually prevent some difficult behavioural problems if your written comments and instructions are clear, easy to read and aimed at the right level. One of the greatest causes of difficult behaviour in the classroom is poor academic self-image. Pupils who are 'Jack-the-lads' outside school can be humiliated in the classroom by their inability to read or understand the work prepared for them.

Any feeling of inadequacy caused by your written communication can be a very significant trigger in producing escalating displacement activities. This can be extreme in lessons where only written instruction is given or where writing is requested in response to instructions without sufficient verbal support and further explanation. You must keep in mind that the child with significant behavioural problems is also likely to have difficulties with learning, decoding and short-term memory.

When presenting written resources or instructions, reading levels should be taken into consideration and the size and type of font used should also be thought about carefully. Not too many words should be placed on the page and questions should be easy to read.

YOUR WRITING SKILLS

PRESENTATION

How you present work to each child and to the class can make the difference between calm and chaos. Children with poor academic self-image and low achievement always have a fear of failure, a wish to avoid work, and a preference for distraction or, if that fails, destruction. So, how you present work and the format you use is crucial to avoid major disruption.

Don't present badly photocopied resources. Make sure that our friends know you have taken a lot of trouble over the preparation of their work. Presenting work to academically and socially challenged pupils has to take into consideration their fears and anxieties about work. Break the work down into bite-sized chunks that are easy to understand and, most of all, exciting to complete. If you yourself are not excited about what you are teaching, how can you expect your pupils to be?

So, to keep these children on side, present your work with care and attention to detail. Use the modern and exciting technologies like interactive whiteboards, DVDs, and the internet which can give a breadth to your teaching that will signal your own interest and enthusiasm for the subject. Everything you present to SEBD pupils must be achievable and worth doing. They must see where the lesson is leading and what success they will achieve by completing the set tasks well.

If things don't go to plan, find other routes to follow. Always have alternative ways of presenting the same lesson. Prepare and have reserve resources and ideas to hand and be aware that changing the content or pace of a lesson can often save your bacon. This might be difficult for inexperienced teachers to achieve initially, but with time and application you will learn to be flexible.

You need to think hard about this point because difficult children will read your body language to gauge your confidence levels and judge how well you think you are coping. If SEBD pupils sense you are under pressure or are feeling defeated by the task, they will be cruel and push you that little bit harder.

Here are one or two things to think about:

○ Stand upright, keep your back straight and your head high.
○ Move calmly and smoothly around the classroom, without making any sudden movements.
○ When approaching pupils, treat the personal space around them with respect. Don't go crowding in too close if all is calm.
○ Avoid tripping up or falling off a chair.
○ Male teachers only – don't fiddle inside your trouser pockets! Children have a name for that kind of teacher!

If trouble does arise, retain the same calm body posture and slow movements, even though inside your stomach may be churning. Don't let your shoulders rise (they will do so at times of great tension), but keep them low and relaxed. Don't clench your fists – this can be seen as a threat or even as an aggressive expression.

BODY LANGUAGE

What have organizational abilities to do with behaviour? The simple answer is a lot. If you are not well prepared, don't have the right number of books or worksheets, challenging pupils will see you as incompetent. You will leave dangerous spaces in your lesson when you are scrambling about looking for equipment that you should have sorted out much earlier. It is often in these spaces that disruptive behaviour begins.

The practical outcome of poor organization will be confusion, time-wasting and resultant chaos. Pupils are sent out for more books, pencils are sharpened, biros fetched. I have seen a lesson destroyed by dried-up felt-tip pens!

So, what should you do (or not do)?

o Preparation, preparation, preparation!
o Your lesson must be watertight.
o Don't slip out of the classroom for forgotten items.
o Bring spare pens and pencils to class for those who have forgotten theirs.
o Don't ask our friends to share books or equipment – they can't share.
o Don't make up a lesson just because you have forgotten a vital component.

These things matter because when our friends see a crack in your defences, they will drive a coach and horses through it.

Your classroom

The single most important thing about your classroom is that it is yours. It is your territory. You may wish to share some aspects of it with your pupils, but the ownership of it must always remain with you.

This is not a selfish or negative notion. The classroom is a special and highly symbolic place, where your skill and craft as a teacher can be displayed on a stage, dressed to enhance all that is good about your profession.

Our SEBDs will recognize this straightaway because they know all about territory – it's one of their specialities. They will be watchful about how you maintain your classroom, how you present it to them and whether you keep it clean and tidy. They will sense whether you are proud of your classroom or don't care about it much. They will test your feelings about its ownership and how you react to it being abused.

Stand your ground and insist that your routines and conventions are respected. Be a good owner of your classroom and show how proud you are of it.

You are very rarely given a classroom fit for purpose unless you teach a very specialist subject and, even then, it is rarely totally appropriate. With SEBD pupils in mind, it is a good idea to think carefully about placement.

○ Where will you stand to present a lesson?
○ Is there an opportunity to develop a teaching wall to act as a backdrop and information centre to your presentation?
○ Will your teaching wall be big enough to display all the essential material required?
○ If you have an interactive whiteboard, are the desks facing the right way for the pupils to see it and can you use the space around the board to enhance the lesson?
○ Do you want pupils to have clear access to the teaching wall? If so, are the pathways between desks and tables clear and is there enough space between them?

If you have potentially violent pupils then think about the following:

○ Where will you place your desk/teaching base in relation to the door? Do you want to be a gatekeeper or allow him to flee unhindered?
○ With some erratic and potentially violent children, an obvious and accessible exit can facilitate escape and might help to avoid a permanent exclusion because the option to take flight is clearly available.

Think about the lighting and acoustics in your classroom. These children can have problems with seeing and hearing. Is the lighting in all parts of the room adequate and can they hear clearly what you are saying? Not being able to hear and understand straightaway can quickly cause panic and disinterest in learning.

CLASSROOM GEOGRAPHY

SEATING PLAN AND MOBILITY

A seating plan is such a powerful tool. The teacher displays to the pupils how she/he is going to manage the social dynamics of the class – placing the pupils where she/he would like them to sit, not asking for views, not yielding to pressure, but simply designing a seating plan that allows the teacher to teach and the pupils to learn.

SEBD children will find this very difficult because they:

o want their friends around them
o want to sit at the back
o want to sit near pupils they like to bully or just annoy
o like to be out of easy reach
o want to sit next to pupils they can control.

This initial plan should not be presented in a challenging way. Just gently state why the seating plan is necessary and why the decisions have been made. SEBDs will object, and may even try to subvert the new order. But be persistent, calm and clear about the purpose of the classroom and the seating plan. Remember, they get a real buzz from being managed fairly. If you give in under protest, then you will lose a foothold in other areas as well. Stick to your guns. Explain why you are doing it and reiterate that the decision has been made and won't be changed.

However, you can set some incentives for the future. For example, tell your pupils that, once everything has been quiet and settled for a number of sessions, then you might consider 'transfer requests'.

Set rules for moving around your classroom, or your 'territory'. Rules for mobility prevent children from moving into areas that will immediately create difficulties. If unrestricted freedom of movement is permitted, the pupils can also subvert the seating plan.

Start by saying, 'No movement around the classroom unless I say so.' This is a clear, easily understood instruction that is simple to carry out. Start with a very tight environment, which is then easy to slacken.

Avoid the opposite approach. The subject being taught obviously affects the amount of movement required. It would be impossible to keep everyone in their seat for PE, but even where mobility is essential to the lesson plan and outcomes it is important to be clear about *where* to move to and *when* to move. Teachers who are most successful with difficult children are those that dare to make clear statements about what will and will not be tolerated. They are also those confident enough both to state the consequences of non-compliance and to carry them out.

If you allow freedom of movement, you will undermine your seating plan; the two go hand-in-hand. In time, you may be able to relax the rules a little but beware – our SEBDs never relax. They may at times look relaxed, but don't be taken in. They are waiting for your next mistake and then they will pounce.

MOVEMENT AROUND THE CLASSROOM

CIRCLE OF FRIENDS

If you have a particularly difficult pupil who constantly irritates the class, you can use the 'circle of friends', a technique that is tried and tested. Many of our difficult children find relationships with other pupils hard. Often their dysfunctional behaviour arises from constant isolation and a sense of hopelessness. They are islands of anger in what is often a sea of tranquility.

Find an opportunity when your difficult pupil is not in the room (even engineer such a time with the help of a colleague). Talk to the rest of the class about the impact his poor behaviour is having. Be sympathetic and understanding about the difficulties the SEBD pupil is having and ask the class for its support. Design a space round the difficult pupil (this could be part of a seating plan) and fill it with understanding and positive pupils. Coach them in responding positively. Ask them to praise his good behaviour and work, laugh at his jokes and not appear threatened by his maladjusted behaviour. If you get the 'circle of friends' chemistry right, it can deliver major rewards for you, the class and, most importantly, the difficult pupil.

The logic behind this is obvious – our friend no longer feels isolated, has support from his peers and is not rewarded for inappropriate behaviour. Ignoring difficult behaviour is a major feature in this strategy. It reduces anxiety in you, in the class and our difficult friend. Furthermore, it diminishes risk of serious incidents breaking out.

Some difficult pupils develop special, trusting relationships with particular adults and do little wrong in their company. This special adult or 'buddy' might be another teacher, a teaching assistant, a senior member of staff, the caretaker, or the groundsman. Get to know the buddy and unpick the chemistry, the dynamics that bind their relationship. What makes it so secure and positive? Enlist the buddy's support.

Ask the buddy:

○ what the difficult pupil likes and hates
○ what the triggers for bad behaviour are
○ whom he likes in the school (staff and pupils) and why
○ whom he hates (staff and pupils) and why (this could be you, of course!).

Get the inside information from the buddy on handling. Find an opportunity to watch the two together and see how they relate to each other. Try to broker a deal with the buddy relating to rewards for good behaviour. Organize extra time for the difficult pupil to spend with the buddy. If appropriate, show the buddy the pupil's report card and arrange for all three of you to sit down and talk over the problems in class. Plan for the three of you to meet the parents and emphasize the areas of good behaviour. Raise the challenging areas of behaviour too, but don't allow these to dominate the agenda.

A PLANNED ALTERNATIVE TO YOUR CLASSROOM

This strategy relies on you having some good colleagues at school who have specific skills in handling our SEBDs. It is about changing the environment immediately following an escalation of challenging behaviour. 'Out you go to Mr A.' Mr A is the one your difficult pupil wouldn't say 'boo' to. This strategy is obviously risky and should be well thought out and planned before being attempted. Mr A has the power, the technique and the experience to reduce your difficult pupil to manageable proportions. The very thought of a 'meeting' with Mr A will make our friend think twice about any sort of challenge to you, and he generally calms quickly. This does of course de-skill you to some extent and should only be used in an emergency.

Teachers, with permission from senior management, have also used this technique to swap difficult children from one class to another for short periods of time. This again takes the wind out of their sails and gets them away from mates, etc. It can be done covertly by sending our friend with a written message to the other teacher or overtly by writing this 'cooling off' option into the pupil's contract. It all depends on the willingness of the other adult to accommodate this arrangement. It must also be understood that this strategy can only be used for a brief period of time. If the 'cooling off' period goes on for too long, the pupil will play the system. It only works if the pupil perceives it as short and sharp.

Rules are a strong and democratic way of managing difficult children, but rules have to be made with a great deal of care. All the pupils affected by the rules should be included in the process. You must generate the right atmosphere in which to develop them, and devote time to the process. They should be based around the need for you to teach your subject in an interesting and uninterrupted way and every pupil's need to be educated in a settled and well-disciplined environment.

Plan a lesson or part of a lesson around rule-building. State clearly why the rules are important and why you want the pupils to participate in the process. Stress the importance of good behaviour and why they, the pupils, should be clear about shared class values. This is an excellent opportunity to include our friends in the discussion. Ask them to express their views openly about what they see as good and bad behaviour. This lesson needs to be handled carefully. Don't allow them too much time but give them a reasonable opportunity to express their views. After all, they know all about rules and how to break them!

Typically, regular pupils like a classroom to be well ordered, relaxed and interesting. They don't like chaos and they hate challenging behaviour from disruptive pupils. So, use this to shape the framework for the rules. Carefully organize everybody's thinking by channelling their ideas into economic statements of expectation – rules, in other words. Get the regular pupils to be clear about the environment they feel comfortable in, but be sure that is in harmony with your need to teach uninterruptedly in a calm environment. Get that balance right and the rules become a powerful tool that is jointly owned by you, the difficult pupil and the whole class.

COMPILING THE RULES

Only develop a small number of rules, between five and eight. A long list quickly becomes boring and irrelevant. Rules should be positive – the dos, not the don'ts. Give SEBDs a line to step over, a wall to knock down.

So, 'Don't talk when the teacher is talking' might be better expressed as, 'When anyone is talking to the class, we should all listen.'

Rules should not be vague. Avoid, 'We should all try to work hard' and replace it with, 'Our class is proud of the standard of work achieved.'

The classic rule to avoid is, 'We must all try to be friends.' This is asking the impossible of any human being! Instead, use a phrase like, 'We expect good manners towards each other in our class.'

Don't make individual rules too long. For example, 'When we come into the classroom and sit down, we should be quiet, allowing the teacher to start the lesson' could be reduced to, 'We expect everyone to be quiet at the start of a lesson.'

Make sure everyone clearly understands the rules once they have been agreed and written down. Deal with any ambivalence or ambiguity at an early stage. Desktop publish the rules and frame them like the Ten Commandments in a prominent place.

Lastly, review them with your co-authors on a regular basis.

There are so many ways of using rules. Make sure the framed copy mounted on the wall is always visible and clean. Give every pupil a copy of the rules and send a copy to all the parents with a return slip attached, instructing the parents to confirm that they have read the rules. Invite them to comment on the rules. If slips are not returned, send a second copy, this time by post. If you are going to have rules and they are to be meaningful, they should be known and accepted by everyone.

You now have a short set of rules that have been unanimously agreed and are owned by everyone. If (or rather when!) SEBDs step out of line, it will not just be against you but also against the will of his own classmates and parents. That's not easy to do because, although his academic self-image might not be high, he often has quite high general self-image. Confronting a teacher might be a worthwhile exercise, but challenging the whole class might not seem quite as attractive a prospect.

Furthermore, with some trigger behaviours you might be able to point to the rules on the wall without saying a single word and the behaviour could subside.

Remember to review the rules regularly to keep them alive and fresh.

USING THE RULES

The lesson

ENTERING THE CLASSROOM

Beginning a lesson punctually is crucial. It sends the message to all your pupils that you as the teacher are ready to start and there is work to be done. First, however, get all the pupils into the classroom and seated. There must be quiet (not necessarily silence) before the class is allowed to enter. Make sure everyone is calm and under control. Start as you mean to go on.

No running, pushing, loud talking or bad language should be permitted during this crucial phase. If any of these occur, stop what is happening and start again. The pupils will tire of this boring repetition well before you do.

Pathways to desks and tables should be unimpeded and understood by everyone. Make sure your seating plans are obeyed.

Then make strong contact with your pupils by reminding them about your expectations at the beginning of lessons. Everyone is expected to be on time, with no latecomers. Remind persistent stragglers of the consequences of lateness. No individual or group of pupils should keep you and the rest of the class waiting. Remind them that being late is bad-mannered, unacceptable and very inconvenient for everyone. Don't begin a lesson by having to recover control.

By doing all this, you are setting out your stall clearly before the learning gets underway.

SILENCE

Once the class is in and settled, gain their full attention. The opening moments of a lesson are vital. Your introduction should be clear, unambiguous and understood, especially by difficult pupils. If they don't know what they are supposed to do they will do something else and that's when big problems begin. If you start an introduction with half the class listening and the other half talking about *Eastenders*, all will not go well for the rest of the lesson.

Work to gain silence, rather than demand immediate obedience; look to reducing the cattle to silence and full attention in a short period of time, thereby avoiding some obvious opportunities for rudeness and confrontation.

'Eyes on me', 'Sit up, please', 'Be still now', a short clapping routine, or everyone standing up are all ways of ensuring that complete silence is achieved. Vary them from day to day, lesson to lesson. The methods for achieving silence at the beginning of a lesson are countless and every good teacher has his/her favourites. If you don't achieve it straightaway, persevere or speak to a colleague. Go and watch other teachers who always start their lessons with silence. Their methods might not be perfect for you, but it will give you some ideas. Experiment with different 'start-of-lesson' routines and hone what is partially successful until it works well for you. Change the form of the ritual. Surprise your pupils.

Silence at the beginning of a lesson is an important marker for all children, not just for SEBDs. However, if the whole class knows and accepts the ritual, the difficult pupils will usually want to conform.

Like a good newspaper article, introduce your lesson with some pertinent, incredibly interesting and amusing remarks. Your aim is to get pupils enthused about your subject, and for that, you must be enthusiastic too – if you're not, then get your tin hat ready.

Try to open with a splash. There are so many aids for teachers now, including multimedia, DVDs, the interactive whiteboard and the internet. Take time in preparing your initial presentation because if it's interesting and engages pupils, it improves their work rate and keeps them on task.

Make sure that the aims of the lesson are clear; make it simple and easy to understand. Beware of the needs of challenging children – most of them will show some interest at the beginning of the lesson and if your presentation does not appeal to them then they will see you as boring and think of other things to do in your lesson, all of which you will not enjoy.

Lesson timing is about the pace you teach at and the way in which you maintain interest and attention in your lessons. The conventional format of an introduction, followed by silent work, before finally closing books and leaving the classroom is not an effective model for any pupils, especially SEBDs. Plan your lessons to have changes in pace and attention span.

- ○ Build in short, interesting breaks.
- ○ Change the delivery medium.
- ○ Follow a writing session with a different activity.
- ○ Break up the style of work.
- ○ Reshape a lesson if things are not going to plan.
- ○ Change the activity or move on to something else earlier than originally intended.
- ○ Be flexible about the work required, but never reduce expectation.

It can be useful to promise something special at the end or in the middle of a lesson. Make contracts with pupils about completion times and the incentives on offer if work is completed well and on time. Find out what is enjoyable for the whole class and remember to include difficult pupils by making sure they can succeed with the activity.

A lesson plan should be a well-designed mosaic that includes:

- ○ careful timing
- ○ changes in pace
- ○ variety
- ○ good learning.

If you achieve that, you will see that the whole class will sustain higher levels of concentration and produce better work. SEBD pupils tend not to work in a linear way and suffer significantly from 'clinical boredom'. You must always keep that in mind.

THE END OF THE LESSON

Your skill in managing your class and the most difficult children can often be measured by how a lesson ends.

○ How will the difficult pupils leave the classroom?
○ Did they enjoy the lesson?
○ Did they learn anything interesting?

Whatever the lesson, finishing in good order is essential. If part of the lesson has been good, these pupils may have a desire to spoil it at the end by being silly or rude. If they were bored, they might want to show their disapproval. Again, their thinking is not always conventional and sometimes paradoxical.

All lessons should have a clear end, when a line is drawn and all work stops. Books, tools, balls, or whatever should be put down or stored away. The final ritual of leaving the classroom should now begin. Difficult children should not be given any chance to stage-manage their exit from the room. They, like everyone else, must comply with the class rules.

All pupils just want to get out of the classroom as quickly as possible to get on with the serious business of school, the corridor and playground chatter! So, use this incentive as a means of controlling the disruptive element.

The weight of the class is a very powerful force at such transitional times in eliminating disruptive behaviour. As the teacher, use this collective power. Wait/ask for or demand silence before allowing the class to leave. Then decide on a ritualistic method for leaving the classroom, but one that again is calm and quiet. Use this moment to make all pupils aware of the power you have as the responsible adult. Make it clear that the class does not leave your territory until it is safe to do so. You don't want to be seen chasing down a corridor trying to recover a lost cause, do you?

What ends well has a good chance of starting well the next time.

High mobility (HM) lessons such as PE or drama are almost impossible for most SEBDs to cope with. They can't handle the space or the pace that these lessons generate and they can't manage the interactions with other pupils.

As a consequence they may:

o look for the children who are easy to pick on and bully
o look for co-conspirators, who will help them create chaos
o run around by themselves just causing problems.

Their behaviour tends to be chaotic because their perception of HM and the consequent freedom it brings is very different from that of the 'normal' pupil.

Their insight tends to revolve round street culture and the deviancy that entails. Lessons such as PE and drama provide temptations they can't resist. As a consequence, for HM lessons these challenging pupils need to be given precise and detailed instructions about what they have to do. They need a programme (with rewards built in) that you have discussed with them and they agree to. If they get A right, then B will follow, and so on. There must always be a carrot, but it must be earned first.

Basic skills

SEBD pupils are always watchful and keep a close eye on what you are doing, where you are in the classroom, and who or what you are looking at. So, it is important for you to be vigilant and aware of:

○ where your pupils are in the classroom
○ who is signaling to whom and about what
○ in particular, what our special friend is doing.

That is a tall order, given that you have to teach as well! Get into a habit of scanning the classroom at regular intervals, using your radar to gather in all the information. It's not difficult, but does require concentration.

Wherever you are standing in the room, glance around, check the difficult pupils, check the class and then go back to what you were doing. If, for example, you are explaining something to one of the pupils, every 10–20 seconds or so look up and just scan round the class and check:

○ if the class is on task
○ who is a bit fractious or distractible
○ if those 'signals' are going round the room about you or another pupil
○ if the more difficult pupils are on task and engaged in appropriate activities
○ if the class is generally settled.

Don't underestimate the power of scanning. Forewarned is forearmed!

If you are diligently scanning throughout a lesson, regular pupils accept and assume that they are under constant scrutiny. They are more mindful about their habits and, as a consequence, the classroom tends to be quieter. Regular pupils are conscious of your attention and tend not to develop inappropriate behaviour as a result.

The more difficult pupils are also aware of your vigilance but that in itself is not enough to control their behaviour. As you scan the room, briefly pause when you alight on your difficult pupil. He may glance back, so use this momentary eye contact to underpin that you are fully alert but are not looking for confrontation. No words have to be exchanged. You might even nod approval or give a slight smile.

Eye contact with our friends several times a lesson will keep the cart on the road. Meet their eye contact with a wink, a nod, thumbs-up, or a smile. However, you must not hold the eye contact for too long as that might be thought of as threatening.

The teacher's scan is a searchlight, spelling out the simple message, 'I am still here and I know what you are doing. I can see all and my light never dims.'

If your light does dim or you stop scanning, guess who will be first to identify your change of behaviour?

CONSTANT VIGILANCE

Using scanning as a preparation for action can save so much pain and suffering for all.

Challenging children tend to gradually build up their disruptive behaviour by responding to triggers and certain types of stimulation. If you have been scanning consistently you will be aware of the escalation and be able to deal with the behaviour in a more proactive way.

Get close to the theatre of action – use your teaching position in the class to reduce tension. Every move, action and instruction by you related to the increased heat should be monitored by further purposeful scanning.

Don't turn your back on the situation, and be constantly vigilant. If the heat does not reduce but stays about the same, keep watching; avoid too long a period of a single eye contact, but increase the frequency.

A single word, even a facial expression, can keep the temperature at a steady but not critical heat. Be on top and keep up the observation. If the problem reduces, withdraw gradually and increase the scanning interval.

Listening or 'audio scanning' is a different but equally crucial skill to learn. A change of background noise in the classroom can be the first warning of trouble. When SEBDs begin to raise the temperature, it is then that the louder, more deviant interactions start, such as:

○ the sharp comment
○ an increase in decibels
○ the quick shriek
○ a burst of inappropriate laughter.

Some of this disruptive behaviour is just aimed at you – to provoke you, test you, see what you are picking up or missing. Are you paying attention? If you are not listening or you don't signal disapproval quickly, then the noise and confusion will increase – more laughter, farts, burps, insults and, inevitably, swearing. If you don't nip these displacement activities in the bud, chaos will ensue and your classroom will become a madhouse.

Keep your ears 'healthy' and your hearing sharp. Listen out for any comments. Correct swearing immediately, but without being aggressive. Just make it clear that you can't accept it in your classroom. Good hearing will mean fewer sleepless nights!

FACIAL EXPRESSIONS AND GESTURES

A typical class of children is fast moving and chaotic, which means it constantly needs to be shepherded. Sub-groups and individuals within sub-groups need to be constantly prompted. But if you are repeatedly asking for quiet, giving verbal instructions and disapproving of behaviour, it will all become a bit of a headache. You will get bored and the class will tire of hearing you. Using facial expression as an alternative can, if done correctly, send out messages that pupils understand equally well.

Your displeasure, disappointment or approval can be expressed without a word being spoken. Think of how at a noisy party or in a busy pub, facial expressions and gestures (movements of the hands, arms and body) are used to communicate important messages. People nod in approval, smile, laugh, frown, point, all as part of their rich tapestry of non-verbal communication.

So, train yourself to use non-verbal communication such as facial expressions and gestures and thereby reduce the need for verbal exchanges, even confrontation, with our friends. The bonus will be that the whole class will benefit.

You do need to practise these non-verbal skills. Yes, it's back to the mirror at home! Develop some appropriate expressions and gestures for:

o disapproval
o annoyance
o pleasure
o bewilderment
o incredulity.

Try them out on your friends or partner. Role-play or mime some scenarios using just facial expressions and gestures. It's surprising how quickly you will become fluent and relaxed about doing this, and it can also be great fun.

School documentation and support

You need to get to know what support the school gives you when you encounter problems with SEBD pupils. This should be contained in the school behaviour policy (SBP) and every school should have one. However, these policies vary in detail and quality.

The SBP should:

o give clear guidelines regarding acceptable and unacceptable behaviour
o state clearly the school's position on physical contact with pupils
o indicate what support the SMT pledges to give individual teachers
o list the records you are expected to keep on incidents and behaviour in general
o detail the responsibilities that parents are expected to take
o give details of all procedures the school expects you to follow.

You need to be sure about the details contained in the SBP. It's a good idea to talk to other teachers about their experiences of support, particularly the procedure for 'call out' when situations become too difficult. For example, who do you call and how do you send for them when you can't leave your class?

Familiarize yourself with the SBP right at the beginning of your contract because making a hash of the first big problem will live with you and others for a long time. Above all, you will lose your self-confidence and the confidence of others.

Because it is difficult to clearly identify specific behavioural disorders, pupils identified as SEBD are not always covered by the school's special needs policy. They are often perceived as just 'social problems' and consequently not always given the protection and potential support of School Action, School Action Plus and, in a minority of cases, a statement of special educational needs.

If your SEBD pupil is giving you a hard time, you need to see if there are any resources allocated in the paperwork that he doesn't appear to be receiving. Resources or resource packages normally contain things like extra classroom assistance, specific procedures when matters get difficult in class, protocols and the school's responsibilities following incidents. Check it out – you may be surprised to find out what you should have been given.

It is the classroom teacher's responsibility to make sure special needs resources and protocols are not forgotten, because a couple of hours of classroom support here or a successful time-out procedure there might help to calm our friends.

STATEMENTS AND IDENTIFICATION OF SPECIAL NEEDS

You need to check the school policy regarding general school mobility. How does the school expect its pupils to arrive at your classroom door? What routes must they take and where should they not go? SEBD pupils seek out the forbidden places, the wrong routes and the gathering points for their like-minded friends. Incorrectly, they believe that being streetwise at school gives them more credibility and kudos with other pupils.

If they are late, ask them to describe their journey to your classroom. Ask for sound reasons to explain their lateness. Routes via the playground and toilets seem to be of special interest to them. Make special rules just for them if problems of punctuality and disturbance arise.

Counteract this behaviour by:

○ delaying their departure from your classroom if they arrive late

○ sitting down with them and getting them to cooperate with the school rules regarding movement (you could even get them to sign a contract regarding movement)

○ talking to other teachers about their movements and trying to 'shut' the alternative routes they regularly find

○ restricting their mobility around the school and giving them less time and space for deviancy.

This might all sound a bit over the top, but if difficult pupils know you are aware of the little tricks they play, they will pay you more respect. They might even see you as streetwise yourself!

Give them a reward if they get it right, but do it surreptitiously otherwise all pupils might all want one.

If you are lucky and have been given support with these difficult children, say in the form of a class support worker or learning support assistant, then this is valuable and must be optimized. The support will vary in terms of quantity and quality.

It is important to develop a good relationship with your class workers. They are an integral and invaluable part of your team and need to be managed effectively and guided in their work. Make sure that you describe in detail the kind of work you want them to undertake and that it fits your purpose and agenda, not those of our friend or the helper him/herself. Be clear about where and how you want your difficult pupil to undertake his work with the support worker. For the pupil's self-image it must be the same or similar to the work being done by the rest of the class.

There are several effective arrangements for supporting an SEBD child:

○ Out of the classroom for short periods of time on a one-to-one basis.
○ Out of the classroom but together with a few regular pupils.
○ In a designated area of the classroom.
○ Within the classroom but with a small group of regular children.
○ With a range of regular pupils but only one at a time.

Much depends on what the difficult pupil can tolerate, how good the support worker is, what facilities are available and what you feel comfortable with.

Remember, if anything goes wrong, it's your responsibility, not your support worker's! So, you have to judge what is best and how to do it.

MANAGING OTHER ADULTS IN THE CLASSROOM

Measuring SEBD

Labels and categories of severity commonly used across all areas of special needs apply equally well to our special friends. For example, the terms 'profound', 'severe', 'moderate', 'mild', even 'multiple' can be comfortably used in describing and measuring SEBD. But how can you measure the degree of difficulty and talk sensibly about the range of the condition?

As a teacher you have the minute-by-minute responsibility in the classroom to manage SEBD children. Consequently, your views, impressions and experience will probably be very different to those of other professionals.

Your own model for defining these pupils and placing them in the categories described above should relate entirely to your job of teaching and your experience in the classroom. So, the amount a pupil disrupts your teaching will automatically place them correctly in relation to your established and tested criteria. The two scales of measurement you could use most are severity and frequency – how difficult a specific behaviour is and how frequently it occurs. When you draw up recording sheets for such measurements they must be carefully thought out and should require a minimum amount of time to complete.

Measuring SEBD in this way will enable you to speak confidently about behaviour and state clearly the degree of difficulty you have to manage. There should be no waffling or subjective pronouncement, just an objective analysis of the degree of difficulty. It also allows you to measure the success or otherwise of any new tactic you employ.

There is a spread of behaviour that SEBD children present to us, ranging from downright impossible to just rather annoying. To benchmark this range, write down a brief description of each behaviour, with the impossible at the top and the annoying at the bottom. Describe behaviours as objectively as possible.

Aim for about 10 or 12 different types of behaviour exhibited across the whole class. Take your sheet into the classroom and tick off each of the described behaviours as they occur. If you need to add more categories or subdivide others, do so. By the end of a week you will have a profile or pattern of the severity and frequency of difficult behaviours in your class.

Now specifically plot the behaviour pattern of your SEBD pupil. His sheet might need to be modified to suit the specific difficulties expressed.

All the sheets you design should be directly related to your job of teaching and how poor behaviour prevents you from teaching and the other pupils from learning.

RECORDING THE BEHAVIOURS

Your records will map the behaviour patterns in your classroom by showing:

o an objective view of what the problems in your classroom are
o how difficult the behaviours are
o how frequently they occur
o at what time of day they happen
o during which lessons.

Your records will also provide a number of direct benefits:

o You can measure our friend's behaviour against the rest of the class.
o You will know when his behaviour occurs and how often.
o You will have a record of the class's response to the difficult pupil's behaviour.

If you collect this information regularly, you will have real data, not tired recollections or subjective memories. As a result, you can improve your teaching programmes, sharpen your management skills and, above all, be more objective and fair about your SEBD pupil's problems. A spin-off might also be that this data provides sufficient evidence for additional SEN support resources to be found.

Using practical measurements of behaviours and behaviour patterns can be intellectually challenging and invigorating. It may give you some insight and impetus. Alternatively, you might just find it all rather irritating and overelaborate, in which case don't do it!

Help from outside

SOCIAL WORKER

There are very few of these pupils that don't have difficult, complicated or unusual backgrounds. That means contact with social services is common. How you might benefit from this contact will vary from child to child, social worker to social worker. It also depends on the extent to which a social worker is already involved. The continuum stretches from a full care order to occasional contact related to the concerns of neighbours, relatives or professionals such as GPs or educational psychologists. Make yourself aware of the pupil's present contact with social services.

If our friend is on a care order, then it is important that you read all the information in his file. Talk to the social worker. Make regular contact with the carers and try to involve them in the management of the child.

If there are matters relating to child protection, then be aware of the problems the child might be facing and monitor any unusual mood swings, anxiety or specific areas of difficult behaviour. Make yourself available if the child wants to talk to you, but be aware of your responsibilities and professional boundaries. Never interview a pupil on your own behind closed doors. You must read the standard procedures for safeguarding the child regarding disclosures and follow the instructions to the letter.

If you are really worried about the child and feel you need advice from a social worker immediately, then with the support of the school express your concerns to the duty social worker. If you are not happy with the response you receive, write down your concerns and, with permission from the SMT, send a letter to the duty team at social services, not forgetting to put a copy of the letter in the child's file. It is important when dealing with social services to keep a copy of all correspondence, conversations and telephone calls. But don't make the mistake of trying to be a part-time social worker yourself!

Services for the class teacher vary from area to area and can be structured in different ways. Find out what support services are available in your area, and if you are having problems with behaviour, get them to come in, observe you at work and talk through issues. Often they are very experienced teachers who have a whole repertoire of skills, and plenty of ideas about what might be happening and what to do.

Behaviour support services tend to be practical and offer down-to-earth advice based on well-tried and successful strategies. Develop a good working relationship with them and use their time not just for specific problems or individual pupils but for whole-school issues.

Talk to your behaviour support teacher about your:

o teaching methods
o classroom management
o approach with specific pupils.

Take time to discuss:

o the dynamics of dysfunctional behaviour
o the causes
o specific disorders or syndromes
o the effect on individuals, the whole class and you as the teacher.

Use your behaviour support team to think through alternative methods of management and different tactics. Try to gain regular times to discuss problems and obtain any materials which might be available.

Learning support services can look at matters concerning pupils' ability to learn and their learning styles. Learning support teachers will be able to offer advice on what additional materials could be used to 'scaffold' our friends' learning, such as methods using:

o differentiation
o writing frames
o alphabet arcs.

Talk to your learning support teacher and find out about different materials you might use, and where the pupil might sit in the class, taking into consideration the quality of his vision and hearing.

EDUCATIONAL PSYCHOLOGIST

Educational psychology has a lot to offer, if you can present a clear picture of the child's behaviour with confidence and professionalism.

It is an analytical discipline, but many educational psychologists have taught in the classroom for at least two years and should have considerable knowledge of the problems you are facing.

Although educational psychologists (EPs) don't pull rabbits from magic hats, they do have access to batteries of tests that can give an insight into the child's learning ability, limitations and, in some cases, other disabilities. Using these tests or assessments, EPs are more able to tap into pediatric resources and specialists from other disciplines. For example, they will have access to visual- and hearing-impaired services, occupational therapists and clinical psychologists. A number of our friends have secondary disabilities that often go unnoticed, and insight into these through other specialists can lead to a greater understanding of the difficulties. With appropriate external support some of their behaviours can be mitigated.

If the EP assessments produce no significant outcomes, your questions have been answered and you know where you stand. If, however, some dysfunctions have been identified, don't waste time, and with the help of the EP, refer to the appropriate agency. If the therapy is corrective then some behaviour problems can reduce – some have even been known to disappear.

Educational social workers (ESWs) are normally attached to the school and concern themselves with attendance and home–school liaison. As many of our friends have problems with attendance, ESWs are useful to get to know and normally have helpful information you can use regarding the home situation. Unlike social workers, their focus is directed at the family's ability to get the pupil to school and the maintenance of good communication between all parties concerned with the pupil's educational progress.

Many pupils with SEBD find school attendance difficult and if they are away for significant periods of time their ability to integrate back into school is often affected. After a period away they have to demonstrate their presence, make a fuss, get into trouble quickly, and then abscond again from school. This unhappy cycle is sometimes repeated time and time again.

The person most helpful with absenteeism is the ESW. Keep him/her informed of any unexplained absences and try to get the pupil back into school as quickly as possible. Although it might be tempting to allow absenteeism to drift on, this is a fool's paradise. Having a rest from our friend is not a good idea and is a form of collusion. The more regular the attendance of the child, the more likely he is to adopt a culture of reasonable behaviour and conformity. Inconsistent patterns of attendance lead to anxiety and ever more difficult behaviour.

As soon as you realize the pupil is not in school, arrange a morning call-up service with the ESW. If possible, encourage the ESW to call in and help the parent to get the pupil into school. You are then expressing support for the parent and an undeniable desire for the pupil to be in school – both of those can mean a great deal to our friend.

EDUCATIONAL SOCIAL WORKER

IDEA

44

The umbrella term 'social, emotional and behavioural difficulties' covers a large number of disorders and needs a variety of different types of support. This includes Connexions (school and careers advisory service), local psychiatric services, youth offending teams (YOTs), the police and voluntary organizations (the so-called 'third sector').

Connexions can be useful for older pupils and can help to resolve problems related to the difficult period of transition from school to adulthood. There is a statutory time allocation for all pupils, which can be forgotten.

Psychiatric services are helpful when these pupils display a variety of behaviours that seem unrelated to their immediate environment. This service is normally accessed through the GP.

YOTs working outside school can often make it easier to handle our friends because they provide a responsible and solid person detached from school to whom the pupil can turn. Call them up and ask for help.

Then there are the community police, who can be a positive, controlling factor too.

Voluntary organizations are available sometimes in the evenings when matters can spin out of control for the child and you get the fallout at school the next day.

Find out what these various support agencies do and contact them yourself from school or, if appropriate, introduce them to your difficult pupil. You will be surprised how helpful they can be.

Communicating with pupils and parents

MAKING A CONNECTION

Many SEBD pupils find communication very difficult. Language has not always developed as well as it does in the regular pupil. Articulation, too, is not always perfect and, consequently, misunderstandings occur. When you get into conversation with SEBD pupils, listen closely and resist taking the lead as you might usually do with other pupils. Don't interject but be prepared to prompt when the conversation breaks down. Resist humiliating statements like, 'What do you mean?' or, 'Get on with it.' Rephrase what you think they might have said when they get tongue-tied.

Avoid the mistake of assuming their utterances are always going to be challenging, and use humour sensitively to repair misunderstandings. Our friends are generally unsuccessful in their communication with most adults and will feel rewarded by your close attention to what they are saying and how they are saying it.

Treat anything positive they say with respect, and listen with intensity. Let them feel they have your complete attention and that you are fascinated by what they are saying (even if you are not!).

Ask them about their own world, their culture, and tell them something about yours. When you fail to understand something, ask them to repeat what they have said (but not more than once as this will just irritate them) or to say it in a different way. Don't pretend to have understood something and then later let the cat out of the bag by showing that you haven't.

By listening respectfully and attentively to all children but especially to these challenging pupils, you make connections and win respect for yourself. This alone takes you halfway to managing difficult children.

Many of these difficult children have disturbed backgrounds and don't experience 'normal' family structures. It is important early in your relationship to identify the main carer(s), their title, surname and status within the family.

There are many categories of carer – for example, parent, step-parent, adoptive parent, foster parent, elder sister/brother, step-brother/sister, aunty/uncle, grandparent, friend of the family, children's home . . . To make things more complicated the carer doesn't have to be, in law, the same person that holds the legal, parenting responsibilities for a child. Nevertheless, it is important that you understand who holds the legal responsibility and know the identity of the carer. You will be hoping that they are one and the same person! For the purpose of this book the carer will be referred to as 'the parent'.

Parenting and caring for our challenging pupils at home is often as difficult as it is in the classroom. Wherever they are, our friends put any adult under great pressure and stress.

When communicating with parents, always be aware of the pressure they are under and the problems they face every day of their lives. Try to work out how the pupil and the parent(s) have arrived at the present situation. Are they inherited difficulties (the parents may have special needs themselves or personal health problems)? Have there been recent major changes or events in the family?

It is important to have a good understanding of the home circumstances and dynamics. There will be times of pressure when a clear picture in your head about the pupil's family background and the players in it will provide critical information.

Make a mistake or say the wrong thing about parenting/home and the lid will blow off what is already a challenging enough situation.

There are many ways in which you can communicate with parents – face to face, by telephone, email, text and by letter. Most parents prefer one particular form of communication that they feel comfortable with. Work out what that is and use it wherever possible. Log any communication you have with the parents, writing brief notes and recording the time and date.

Make a point of sending positive messages home whenever possible. Relate these to immediate things such as a good piece of work completed, consistent attendance at school (even if the behaviour has not been good), correct dressing for school, not smoking at school, or a good report from another teacher. Communicating regularly using the parents' preferred medium will help the parents feel good about their child, at least in the context of school. Doing this will build a professional relationship and a bank of trust, which will come in useful when unpleasant but necessary messages have to be sent home.

When things are not going well for these children at school, ensure that parents are consistently aware of particular incidents. Start the conversation or written communication with references to the better times. Show respect and understanding for the parents' position and leave plenty of time and space for them to respond.

Don't judge and condemn the child's behaviour but state the facts of the incident clearly and substantiate details of what occurred. Antagonism, aggression, or criticism of parenting must be avoided at all cost, especially at such delicate times when, invariably, the parents will defend their child's actions and behaviour.

However, remain clear and precise about the consequences of the incident and give the parents full details of any procedure that might have to be followed . Don't collude with the parents against the school or a particular member of staff because therein lies the road to ruin.

Meetings are crucial for your future mental health and the class's ability to learn. Make a joint decision with the parents of a difficult child about the pupil's attendance at and involvement in the meeting. Decide if the pupil should be there for the whole or part of the meeting. Perhaps there should be a time during the meeting just for the adults to talk? Do not underestimate the importance of any meeting with parents. Prepare for the meeting with care and attention to detail. Make a checklist of what you should do before the meeting starts.

A few of the following could be included in your own checklist:

○ Ensure that the SEBD pupil's school files are on the table (remember these are open files).
○ Make available all documents relating to a particular incident or incidents.
○ Have individual education plans, behaviour contracts and all documentation relating to the pupil's special needs status to hand.
○ Have examples of work, completed or not, to refer to.
○ Provide essential class records that relate to day-to-day behaviour.

Also:

○ Make sure you have a suitable meeting room.
○ Depending on the seriousness of the incident, check that all the appropriate people can attend the meeting. Typically, these will include some of the following: SENCO, member of the SMT, head of year, educational psychologist, ESW and, if the child is subject to a care order, the allocated social worker.
○ Offer tea, coffee, biscuits and make water available to set a non-confrontational tone to the meeting.

It is essential that you:

○ make the parents feel welcome
○ treat them with courtesy and respect
○ make it clear to all concerned what the meeting is about, who is chairing it, how wide ranging it will be, including, if appropriate, a carefully veiled reference

(not as a threat but as a serious option) to the
possibility of exclusion
o are clear about the agenda and the time constraints of
the meeting
o ask in advance that the meeting should finish with
everyone still present.

Once you get meetings with parents right, they can be of
enormous therapeutic value and act as a relief valve.

Challenging behaviour and triggers

Triggers are those small external events which are tolerated by the regular pupil but cause anxiety and inner turmoil to SEBDs.

When we are tired after a hard day at school and things just don't work out right, we get irritated by the slightest event. These trivial incidences make us quite angry. Well, it's no different for challenging children, except that their nerves are frayed just about all the time, especially when they are at school and when things appear to go against them.

In a state of heightened tension they are vulnerable to quite small stimuli and changes. They react disproportionately to minor incidents and, if you don't react immediately, their poor behaviour will quickly escalate.

o At the beginning of every lesson scan the room and check how settled our friends appear.

o Are they already reacting irritably to people around them?

o Are they upset by something beyond their immediate environment and across the room?

o Or are they quieter than usual (never a good sign!)?

It's a bit like watching a float when fishing; any little dip or movement sideways warns you about what's going on under the water!

When challenging children are disappointed by something, it tends to be acute and there is very little middle ground. They firmly believe in the adage that 'It's no good being second because you are always the first of the losers.' They have high (impossible) expectations but low ability and poor application. This is a disastrous recipe!

Find out quickly what they are disappointed about. Is it:

○ difficulties at home
○ a bad encounter with a girlfriend/boyfriend
○ a present they really wanted but didn't arrive (some new clothes, a DVD, etc.)
○ a poor outcome from a big effort?

Don't be too direct in making your enquiries. Be subtle and kick one or two ideas around quietly with the pupil. Normally he will spill the beans and will be pleased, indeed relieved, to divulge the problem. When you get to the bottom of the problem, play its seriousness down a bit but promise to give it time later, say, after the lesson or at lunchtime. Whatever you do, don't break your promise by failing to find the time.

During the lesson, keep one eye on the disturbed pupil, giving him an occasional glance, but make it low key.

DISAPPOINTMENT

NEGATIVE REINFORCEMENT

When SEBDs are feeling sensitive (which is most of the time) and they commit a small misdemeanour at the beginning of the lesson, don't draw immediate attention to it with a public reprimand. This is especially important if it is the first time you have communicated with the pupil in the lesson. Maybe you have forgotten to greet him warmly on arrival.

Avoid reinforcing negative behaviour by drawing attention to it and increasing the probability of it reoccurring. However, make sure the pupil is aware that you know what has happened. There are times when minor incidents are better ignored or just marked by a glance. After all, the pupil is probably just testing your nerve and patience. And, of course, as a good teacher you have infinite nerve and patience!

Often teachers follow an opening reprimand with another in quick succession if compliance from the pupil is not immediate. This can be irritating, and bad behaviour can then escalate rapidly. Give a little take up time; once you have asked for compliance just pause and wait for the pupil to respond. This is simply allowing a few seconds to elapse following your glance or gesture. Give him time to settle and not feel threatened by your first request for better behaviour. There is a thin and subtle line between jumping in too quickly and not reacting quickly enough – it's all in the timing.

We all carry concerns and fears about future events – a sick relative, an overdue mortgage repayment, even something as trivial as facing a difficult meeting. These challenging children have concerns too but of a much more acute nature – future sexual abuse, a relative released from prison, a parent leaving home, going back into care, or coming out of care and going back home.

When such major events occur, teachers have to be very careful and strategies for behaviour management need to be more covert. If you are aware of a forthcoming event that might be traumatic for our special friend, have a plan of action ready so that, if/when the behaviour begins, you can quickly take him to another place in the school.

○ Teach very close to the pupil and monitor his behaviour carefully, rewarding whenever possible.
○ Ask him to help another teacher in a much younger class.
○ Ask him to do a job with another adult outside the class that simply must be done now.
○ Get cover for your class and take time out to talk about the anxieties the pupil may want to discuss.

This all sounds a bit dramatic, but by pre-empting a situation you might actually be able to prevent a frightening moment or major incident.

SOMETHING BAD IS GOING TO HAPPEN

When you make a promise to these children, never break it. So, be careful what you promise. However, sometimes in this imperfect world, things happen that are simply beyond a teacher's control. For example:

o The football pitch is flooded and the match is cancelled.
o The DVD player is broken.
o Lunch is late because of a power cut.
o A trip out has to be cancelled because snow has closed the roads.
o The headteacher has changed the timetable and the pupil's favorite lesson has been cancelled.

Even in the best run schools these things happen and in most cases the regular pupil just accepts the consequences as part of the fabric of life. Not so the SEBD child! He, paradoxically, expects perfection, certainty and predictability in others.

How does a good teacher mitigate this potential disaster?

o Work as hard as possible to prevent any change in the first place that you know will cause disappointment.
o Have something exciting in reserve.
o Explain clearly what has happened and why it is outside your control.
o Explain the changes that have to be made to the challenging child before you tell the rest of the class. This will make him feel all the more important and you will be more likely to gain his respect and understanding regarding the disappointment.

If you don't get this right, the situation may escalate and disaster won't be far away!

These difficult children generally do not thrive in an educational environment and have very poor academic self-images. Whenever this inadequacy is exposed and reinforced, a defense mechanism follows. So, how you teach, praise and mark written work must take these factors into consideration.

Here are some examples of teacher behaviours that can create problems:

○ Big red crosses in books and on worksheets.
○ Sarcastic and unpleasant remarks on written work.
○ Unnecessarily personal remarks in front of other classmates.
○ The public announcement of test results.
○ Sorting out problems of school dress in front of the class.
○ Public criticism of a haircut, a pair of trainers, etc.
○ General humiliation.

Remember:

○ Work should be marked.
○ Bad behaviour must be corrected.
○ Test results should be known.

But it must all be done with subtlety and sensitivity. Get it wrong and you know what will happen! Your ego as a teacher must stay intact but not at the expense of someone who cannot defend theirs. Think carefully about how and when you criticize these difficult children.

Don't create a problem and then blame it on the pupil.

Pre-empting escalation

It is safe to assume that SEBD pupils are always vulnerable in school – they often fear the work, another pupil or you. They often exist in a heightened world where being on top and in control are crucial to staying safe.

They are therefore always sensitive to anything and anyone who challenges their place in the group. Within them this sensitivity is deep-rooted and you should accept that and manage it to the best of your ability.

Therefore it is preferable to pre-empt the behaviour and stop the escalation rather than have to deal with the consequences of a full-blown incident.

o Never relax with challenging children.
o Accept that their condition rarely improves significantly.
o Realize that they are the key to a peaceful class.
o Learn about their habits, likes and dislikes.
o Be adaptable and set up flexible systems to manage the unexpected.

Be prepared, watchful and diligent, not just occasionally but all the time you are managing these children. Initially, survival is a success; eventually, learning might be possible.

Giving attention is a subtle and difficult art and one that comes with practice coupled with awareness. As we know, these children are constantly on the edge of chaos and resolve many problems with aggression.

The classroom they work in needs to be a well-maintained environment with routines, expectations and good positive relationships underpinning it. This is something they are normally not familiar with at home.

When you see escalation beginning, that is the time to give positive and supportive intervention. Be careful to start in a low key manner – a glance, a positive remark, a reprimand to someone else nearby but someone who can take it.

Teach nearby, talk to your difficult pupil about unthreatening, non-work-related subjects such as pop music, football or TV. Appreciate his opinions and, where possible, praise him. Then, seamlessly, return to the subject you are teaching as though it was all just a natural continuity of the lesson.

Be flexible, talk about successfully completed work or good behaviour and work from earlier in the lesson. Find something positive to say and smile.

Get this technique right and you can use and reuse it to build a successful early warning system enabling calm de-escalation.

MANAGING OTHER PUPILS

Sometimes, the escalation of behaviour can be brought about by the interaction between two or more pupils. Our friends are easily led and easy to wind up. There are some pupils who are not in themselves hard to manage but will always enjoy a spectacle and will go out of their way to develop one. They are the fringe players, who hover and engineer potential disasters unless checked by you early on.

They are not as sensitive or vulnerable as the more challenging children, so you can be much more direct with them. Make it quite clear that you are aware of their intentions and that you won't tolerate their behaviour. Make it perfectly clear what the consequences of their behaviour will be. They will, no doubt, proclaim their innocence and perhaps even complain that you're picking on them. Ignore this subterfuge. It is just designed to distract you.

Make them sit well away from your SEBD pupil and out of eye contact. If they come into class as a group, split the group up straightaway and don't allow networks to reform. If, after being warned, they make remarks that are likely to provoke, jump on them from a great height, offering no second chance.

Always be fair and keen to prevent injustices because all the pupils in your class will admire and respect you for that.

SEPARATING PUPILS

There are dynamics in some escalations that can be prevented with a bit of careful pre-empting. Who sits where and with whom is crucial in all classrooms. When certain pupils sit together, expect the storm clouds to arrive. Once they have sat down together, it is very difficult to separate them. Be clear and consistent about why pupils are not allowed to sit together in your class, and don't change your mind.

However, if the unexpected happens and pupils need separating, you have to think quickly and work out what is achievable and what is not. Damage limitation might be the better part of valour. For example, choose the pupils that are malleable to your management and get them to move first. Stand close to the pupils and quietly insist they move. If necessary, move their books and equipment to the new places and wait for the reluctant pupils to follow. Stay calm and keep quietly insisting:

o Could you move to your new place please?
o I have moved your books, can you please follow them?
o Could you please move?
o Could you move please . . .?

Avoid, 'If you don't move now I will . . .' because you are setting up a negative target for the pupil to achieve.

The move may take some time to achieve but is well worth the effort. Although some pupils may continue to cause problems, you have made your point and set your precedent. Seating arrangements for the next lesson will be easier to organize.

CHANGING ACTIVITY

Some lessons don't always go to plan. They might be badly designed, poorly thought out, have insufficient work, or are not possible because of the dynamics of the class. As we all know, 'he who hesitates is lost'. This is no hollow cliché when it comes to working with our SEBD pupils. If you are going to change an activity in a lesson because it might reduce tension, then prepare for it, make the transition smooth and ensure that your instructions are easily understood by all the pupils.

There should be:

o no milling about
o no confusion
o no gap before the next load of equipment is ready
o clear seating arrangements
o only minimal handing out or collecting in of work.

Research shows clearly that a return to previous work, just because the teacher forgot something, will seriously damage the lesson and the class's perception of the teacher's management skills. The more challenging pupils hate going back and they hate incompetence and confusion. It makes them anxious and nervous.

So, once you have made the change, you can't go back. Finish that work another day, in another way.

Most SEBDs have low performance skills. Their ability to study, absorb information and organize data is normally very poor. When faced with a class test, they panic, see potential failure and pull out in any way they can.

Preventing this specific escalation can be difficult because tests, informal and formal, are the bread and butter of school life. However, there are various options you might like to consider:

○ Avoid whole-class testing whenever possible.
○ Redesign how a test is administered – test small groups of pupils at different times of the week/term and have them supervised by another adult.
○ Differentiate the content of non-statutory tests so that our friends have a feeling of success and achievement (but make sure all tests look the same!).
○ If possible, make tests shorter and praise the difficult pupils for their good behaviour.
○ Make testing an integral part of everyday teaching, not a special event. This gives the perception that they are no different from, or more important than, other forms of learning.

In summary, monitor and redesign what you test, how you test and for how long. If testing is essential, do it but be wary of the pitfalls.

Behaviour likely to escalate

KEEPING BUMS ON SEATS

Challenging children, if they are ignored, can often get out of their seats and roam the class to cause trouble. This behaviour will always cause problems. They can be isolated in the class because of their behaviour and consequently they search out human contact, which is almost never helpful.

If this is a constant problem, talk to the pupil out of the classroom environment, explain the problems it can cause and ask for support.

○ Seat him in a place in the class where roaming is difficult and easily corrected.

○ Watch him out of the corner of your eye and at the first movement away from the desk ask what the problem is and get alongside him quickly.

○ Make sure the movement out of seat is not encouraged by other pupils, and view any support for this behaviour with disdain.

○ Make a general announcement about moving out of seat at the beginning of every session, and ensure that the rule is clear and meaningful.

○ Make sure *all* the pupils know why you insist on the rule.

This is a classic – if you can't do the work, stop everyone else working. You can see the logic in that, so what do we do about it?

○ Place SEBDs as far away as possible from anyone who is likely to respond aggressively or may be vulnerable to bullying.
○ Deal immediately with any abusive remarks aimed at particular pupils.
○ Keep reiterating the conditions under which the class works and refer constantly to the work in hand.
○ Try to spend as much time as possible standing by challenging children, constantly and positively prompting them regarding their own progress.

If there is a particular exchange between two pupils which is causing harm to the class's progress, then if possible take them outside the classroom. Deal with the problem clearly, stating why such behaviour must not continue. One of the best deterrents is to suggest that if the behaviour does not stop you could meet them both after school to get a better understanding of their problems. If it persists then perhaps a meeting should be arranged with both sets of parents.

It will help in these difficult times if our challenging pupil can actually read what is required and can complete the work given (see Idea 8, Your writing skills).

HINDERING OTHER CHILDREN

Every time you open your mouth he jumps in and makes a silly remark. Ask a question and our friend gives you a silly response. He is trying to take control of the class and make you look a fool, so what do you do?

First, you have to appear to be confident about the management of the behaviour and quick witted enough to out-gun him. He wants chaos and control by humiliating you, and the more early ground he makes, the more laughs, the weaker your position. Therefore, you have to watch out for the first sign of the behaviour. Don't always try to match the humour, but point out the stupidity and ask politely for the behaviour to cease as it is hindering the class's progress.

Depending on the situation and the behaviour the pupil is capable of, you could ask him to come up to the front and open the lesson. There are obvious risks to this tactic but that's where your judgement comes in. Alternatively, you could ask him to spend some time after school with you preparing the next lesson.

You have to be quick, accurate and specific, with no hesitation. Practise this art at home. Get a friend from home to shoot quite abusive remarks at you and try to respond with clear, amusing (not humiliating) reposts. Try cooking a meal and get someone to make stupid remarks about how you are preparing and cooking the food. Deal with it without humour but by skilfully managing the remarks aimed at you. Keep the game going, keep calm, mind your voice doesn't wobble, and make direct eye contact, but only when you speak.

Now go back into the classroom and do the same – stand tall, be strong and confident but not arrogant. If you get it right, he will become quieter.

Threatening other children is against the law and must be taken very seriously in your classroom. Although your classroom is inside a school, it is still part of the wider world and that must be made clear to all challenging children. Threatening violence or actual violence is a criminal offence and should be viewed as such. You must make that clear to the whole class.

Threatening, like most other similar behaviours, has a pattern of testing first and then, if not controlled, escalating. Difficult children love to posture and appear threatening. Most of the time that's as far as it goes, but try to snuff it out right at the beginning.

Initially, the threat can be almost a joke – watch out for this one and intervene immediately in a low-key way but with clarity.

Often it won't go away – remarks related to future encounters are often made at this point. Don't let it go. If necessary, write down the remark and read it back quietly to the pupil and say that this is a criminal offence and you are debating what to do with the information. Make it clear that in your classroom this behaviour will not be tolerated.

SEBDs will try other sly methods of announcing their physical threat. Whenever this occurs, deal with it, not aggressively but quite coldly. Make it plain you understand the threat which has just been made and will note each incident.

THREATENING OTHER CHILDREN

MAKING A NOISE

Making a noise such as banging a desk is a way of expressing frustration. The pupil has lost any connection to the lesson and is warning you about his isolation. It might not look like that because it can often be done with a smile, even a laugh. Research has shown that although other children might be laughing they are not amused, but peer pressure suggests it's better to laugh than ignore it. The regular pupil just wants you to stop the behaviour.

You have to be careful with the tactics you employ here because our challenging pupil is frustrated and wants class attention, or possibly class domination.

You could ask everyone to stop working and listen to the noise or banging, even ask the pupil to try a bit harder while everyone listens. Move close and say, 'That was great. Now can we all get on and I will help you to get back on track.' Again, you have to stand tall, be calm, speak quietly (with perhaps a touch of menace) and don't mince your words.

Another approach with desk banging is to sit on the desk yourself, start to talk about the work in hand, with a smile and a tinge of amusement regarding the behaviour. This is difficult to do when your heart is beating quite fast.

Another tactic would be to have a break in the lesson already prepared and show, say, a related DVD or an internet site on your interactive whiteboard, breaking the flow of the lesson and hopefully the poor behaviour. Technology is a great aid to behaviour control because it adds a very significant number of tactics you can use to not only distract but even amuse and, if you are on the ball, actually teach our friends.

Rudeness in general gets worse if allowed to go unchallenged; difficult pupils will go up the swearing/ obscenity ladder until they reach the very top. It would be sensible to pick up any deviancy right at the bottom of the ladder. This can include overfamiliarity, words whispered so you can just hear them, and the classic mispronunciation of common swear words, followed immediately by, 'But I didn't say that.'

What you have to do is be alert, open-eared and quick in response to any of the above, and don't let it grow. At the same time, don't nag – that is just very amusing to these pupils.

Try not to use the word 'swearing' because in a sense it reinforces the behaviour. You could use such terms as epithet, sexualized language or obscenities. It might just change the way the behaviour is thought of.

This is a difficult skill to learn. The real trick is to ensure that from the very first time you take a new class, you do not allow rudeness of any sort. Make it absolutely clear that rudeness and bad language are totally unacceptable.

Don't, whatever you do, try to be trendy and swear yourself – that would make your position as a teacher very vulnerable.

RUDENESS AND SWEARING

CAUSING MINOR DAMAGE

Behaviour involving minor damage to equipment, furniture or the pupil is quite challenging because, generally, the pupil is sending out signals of distress. The ripped books, broken compass, paint on clothing and broken pen with ink everywhere are telling you that anger has crept into the behaviour. If you want to prove that statement, just shout straight in the face of the pupil and tell him he did it on purpose, then you will see raw anger straightaway.

When anger is creeping in you have to become very calm, try a slight smile and try to put everything right. Initially, it's not a good idea to start talking about reparation – just get on with putting it right.

○ Replace a damaged book with a new one and make a point of smoothing the pages of the old one.
○ Provide a new compass and make a display of trying to repair the old one.
○ Send out for spare clothing or keep spare clothes in the classroom, and make remarks about staining.
○ Provide a new pen and perhaps a wet wipe to clean up hands.

This is all about calming – the consequence comes later. At the end of the lesson, ask the pupil to stay behind and put the book back together, straighten the compass, take the clothes that are soiled and put them in a bag with a note home about how it happened.

If, however, the damage continues after your calming tactics then you have to be more forceful. You might ask why he is damaging everyone's equipment and perhaps suggest that replacing the item might be costly for his parents. Be clear about cost and consequence.

Treat this behaviour with care as it is very easy to blow the situation wide open.

Now, this is a tricky one to work with. The best way of avoiding a refusal to comply is, of course, to make no demands, but that's just a road to an abdication of responsibility. Demands have to be made and responded to appropriately, otherwise the pupil's power is just increased and he can dominate the classroom.

At home and in public places these challenging pupils often refuse to comply; they tend to use anger and violence, usually getting their way. So, you have to be skilful and perceptive.

The trick is in how you ask the question and when:

HOW

○ Well-mannered requests are often not refused.
○ Demands, the purpose of which are clearly stated and requested with a smile, often work.
○ Requests, quietly spoken and gently repeated until complied with, can work.
○ Making it clear that the demand is fair and applies to all is a good tactic.
○ Asking a group which has our friend as a member to comply often gets results.
○ Being completely clear about what is expected is essential.

WHEN

○ Give warning of the expectation.
○ Make it clear at the beginning of the lesson exactly what is expected.
○ Find a time when the pupil seems to be calm and communicative.
○ Try to make demands when you are having a positive and reasonable conversation.

REFUSAL TO COMPLY

THROWING THINGS

Throwing things is a very difficult behaviour to deal with, especially in lessons where the materials can be broken into small pieces. It is not just challenging children who enjoy throwing things about the classroom, but they see it as great fun, an opportunity to be very disruptive, and they don't know when to stop.

As with most behaviours, it is best to catch it early, at the first sign – a big display of disapproval by you and perhaps it will go away. If, however, it becomes a significant behaviour, either by neglect on your part or the determination of certain children, then you have to do something quickly.

○ Make everyone stand up and clearly state what the consequences are if the behaviour continues.
○ Collect in any material that could be used as a missile and make the lesson a written one.
○ If the objects are made from paper, collect in all the books/paper and wait for a stated period of time, which you could then take off their breaktime.
○ Make a big fuss of any damage either to a pupil, yourself or property which was caused by a flying object.
○ Stop the class and be clear about the health and safety aspects of such dangerous behaviour.
○ At the beginning of the next similar lesson give clear warnings about the consequences of throwing things and have a lesson prepared which does not give any throwing opportunities.

A temper tantrum means life can become very difficult, not just for you but also the class. The pupil reaches a state of such anxiety and stress that the only possible outlet is a full temper tantrum.

A temper tantrum could best be described as a major regression. That, however, may be part of the key to prevention. Most regressions start with initial warnings of intent, such as:

o silence and withdrawal
o hiding under a desk or in a corner
o manic repeating of words or phrases.

Be aware of what could possibly happen and get the challenging child either into a safe place or out of the room altogether. Don't refer to his behaviour – he is aware of what is happening – just use an excuse, make a false statement and get him out of there.

That might appear a bit drastic (well it is) because if you allow the tantrum to flower you really are going to require the strength and nerve of the whole SMT to resolve not only the problem but the possible damage incurred as a result. You must spot temper tantrums before they get going – if not you will require special training, which should include advice on physical management.

THE TEMPER TANTRUM

Interventions following escalation

CAN YOU MANAGE THE BIG CHALLENGE?

Even with the most competent teachers these challenging children will still push beyond what is manageable by the tactics described so far in this book.

Once the situation starts to escalate then the pupil's ability to manage his own behaviour diminishes. He becomes anxious, even more sensitive, and his behaviour can become erratic. These are dangerous times and you must tread very carefully.

This is where not only knowledge of the pupil's dysfunction is essential but also some understanding of your own capabilities is required.

The most appropriate comparison is that of a member of the emergency services dealing with a difficult and sometimes dangerous event. They cannot afford to be emotional; they are simply required to do their job. That's what you have to do – deal with what is presented, no shirking. Follow the protocols of the school regarding dangerous and profoundly challenging behaviour.

o If you don't know what to do, ask for some training.
o If you don't want to do it, ask for a quieter job.

These difficult children will occasionally go for the big time and you have to cope with it. If you are successful when things get tough, put the experience in the bank and think through what you did, why it was successful, and then treat yourself to something really nice.

If it wasn't successful, think hard, ask for help, modify your technique and try harder next time.

If angry children are not protected from triggers created by other pupils in the class then their negative behaviours are likely to escalate. They are like an empty castle; once the defences have been breached it becomes weak. That weakness pinpoints the disability, and consequently the anxiety increases and the behaviour becomes more dangerous. You now have two problems – our friend's increased anger and the success felt by the pupil or pupils causing the problem.

There is perhaps just one solution – get the pupil out of the firing line while allowing him to maintain his dignity. Get him out of the room – ask him to fetch something, take a note, collect some material or go to a prearranged place for time-out. Then deal with the pupils who are winding him up. You could be quite forceful and perhaps talk about possible consequences if their behaviour reoccurs.

If you don't divide the two behaviours but try to deal with them simultaneously, the protagonists could be negatively reinforced, our friend even more outraged and the awful situation could become much worse.

TRIGGERS CONTINUE

Sometimes none of your calming tactics work. If you have some understanding of the profound nature of the pupil's disability and your relationship is not strong enough to manage the escalating situation, get him out of the classroom.

There should be a clear school policy on his removal and if the child is profoundly disturbed there must be a specific 'handling policy' for that pupil. Don't forget to check the paperwork on all these really difficult pupils, and the availability of outside help.

The skill is in knowing you are going to be defeated, predicting the possible outcome and preventing the maelstrom. It is not a good idea to be brave in these situations, so invoke the 'handling policy' sooner rather than later and a more serious incident might be avoided.

It might be helpful to make clear to the pupil what you are doing and why. If you choose to do that then you must be quiet, determined and clear about the consequences of the specific behaviour; stay calm and resolute.

This is obviously easier said than done, but if you get your behaviour right there is a chance the challenging child will recognize your strengths and comply with your wishes.

The increased frequency of a behaviour is often a measure of the speed of escalation. If whatever you are doing to dampen down the behaviour is not working, beware – it will soon evolve into something quite unmanageable.

So, think quickly – you don't have much time to change your tactics:

O Are you nagging?
O Are you ignoring (this is not the time to ignore)?
O Are you shouting repeatedly at the pupil?
O Are you confused and not doing anything?

There are such a variety of responses as the behaviours are rooted in different antecedents, but you must try to resolve things at this stage before they reach tipping point.

Don't just go on with the same tactic and then blame the child for all the problems. Make a fresh assessment and change tack. You can do this quite quickly, even surprising the pupil with the change. This is quite a high risk, high energy solution.

You can change tack with a bit of humour and say why you are behaving in a different way.

It is possible to calm behaviour at this stage by using your agility, perception and knowledge gained from previous situations. Be flexible, easy to read and appear confident at all times.

INCREASING FREQUENCY OF A BEHAVIOUR

PERSONALIZED INSULTS

When thing aren't going right for challenging pupils they can often resort to insulting language and remarks aimed at you. Some teachers can become quite subjective about this, but that is a road to ruin.

The child is in a corner, back against the wall, and he sees you as the main cause of the problem. You must remember that these pupils see very little wrong with their behaviour. They tend to externalize the problem, and your incompetence, stupidity, inadequacy, even your personality or personal appearance, are the cause of *all* the difficulties. Keep those thoughts in mind when attempting de-escalation.

You might like to try one or more of the following statements:

o Ok, you're right, so let's just get on.
o I find your remarks interesting, but a bit hard. We all have faults. Now where were we?
o You know that's not true, so let's stop the rubbish and concentrate on the work.
o You said that last time – either find something new, try a bit harder, even write it down so I can read it later, or get on.
o Now, let me see, you have just said, '★★★★ ★★ ★★★★★★'. Let me write that down so we can all remember it. I didn't quite catch it all, so can you repeat it please? Perhaps your parents might like to read it later?
o I think maybe we have all had enough. Can you say everything you have to say and then the rest of us can get on?
o Shut up (sometimes this can work).

Gradually increase the opposition and watch out for the reactions, building on what goes well.

Crisis time

FROM ESCALATION TO CRISIS

So what can be done when you have not prevented the escalation and the challenging child is very anxious, making negative choices and is in crisis? It is important that you:

○ stay safe
○ think about the consequences of your behaviour
○ understand more about the dynamics of behaviour.

Any mistake at this time can cause the behaviour to run very quickly out of control. You have to remain calm and have a quick mind, ready to grasp any opportunity to settle the behaviour.

You need to be aware of:

○ what you are capable of managing and tolerating
○ how supportive the school is regarding the class's safety and your personal well-being
○ how proficient the school support services are when things get tough.

When a challenging child reaches a state of high tension you have to listen very carefully to what he is saying because somewhere in the middle of the shouting and mumbling is a clue.

Pay attention to everything that is being said, don't pass judgement, but occasionally ask for a bit of calm and clarity.

There may be swearing – don't demand it should stop, but ask if it could be lessened. If you make any outright demands, they will become the problem and create a focus for the anxiety.

Make sure you keep to the cause of the anger and give assurances that it can be solved, but only in a calm and well-mannered way.

Throughout this process it is advisable to move closer to the pupil but avoid any touching and stay at a distance that feels comfortable to both of you. Keep reminding him that no one has been hurt and the problem will be solved.

Normally, distressed pupils' anxieties will go in waves, so don't expect a smooth journey – wait for the small waves and use them to assure our friend that all is safe.

At the same time, you must retain contact with the rest of the class and maintain the momentum of the lesson. Be especially wary of other pupils in the class who like dramas and provoke our friend – those pupils can be asked to wait outside until calm is restored.

As things calm down, increase your contact with the class but maintain clear contact with the difficult pupil as little bubbles of anger can still appear from time to time.

DEFUSING

MANAGING YOUR RESPONSES UNDER PRESSURE

When SEBDs are in this crisis phase it is important that you get the style and tone of your speech correct. When these difficult occasions arise your pulse quickens, your blood pressure soars and this can affect your speech.

Try to speak slowly, control your breathing and pronounce your words carefully. By speaking slowly you are expressing the seriousness of the situation but also it gives you time to think and plan what comes next because any inappropriate remark or too heavy an emphasis on obedience can cause a major disruption.

When the pupil is beginning to lose control, he is listening to your enunciation and the vocabulary you are using to assess the level of stress he is causing in you. Any sign of anxiety or stress in your voice can only heighten the chances of a further, more dangerous challenge.

Keep calm, plan what you are going to say and measure from the responses you get how appropriate your verbal intervention is.

By displaying extreme behaviour, difficult pupils are trying to dominate their immediate environment. This is often caused by insecurity and a sense of desperation, although it may appear to be otherwise. Just remember, these children can often seem quite paradoxical.

Eye contact is a major factor at this stage of the challenge; too much direct eye contact may appear to be too significant a confrontation. The pupil may see it as a direct challenge from you and respond forcefully, which is not what you want at this stage.

Try to keep your eyes calm and their normal shape – no wide-eyed glares or nasty narrow eyes. You must have eye contact otherwise it will be assumed that you are weak and perhaps frightened by the behaviour. Therefore, at this crisis stage, you must strike a suitable balance.

○ Use eye contact to emphasize a phrase or an important statement you make.
○ You could reserve intermittent eye contact for when the pupil is speaking, but do not use continuous eye contact.
○ You can give random eye contact which, if done carefully, can reduce anxiety.

Be aware that he will be watching your eyes and how you use them to measure your attitude.

KEEPING CALM EYES

AVOID WIN OR LOSE SITUATIONS

Often at times of crisis SEBDs will try to push you into win or lose situations. Their behaviour becomes excessive and they want you to demand that it stops. They would like you to say things like:

○ Leave the room immediately.
○ Stop swearing now.
○ Sit down in your own chair now.
○ Just be quiet.

In a less stressed situation these demands are perfectly reasonable, but in a crisis they may lead to disaster. Specific demands which require immediate obedience are just what he was planning for. The response is very predictable, 'Are you going to make me then?'

Try to use phrases like:

○ It would be a good idea to stop doing that.
○ It might be better if you stopped doing that.
○ If you could just sit down I will try to sort it out.
○ You have a good point, but I am not sure I can agree with all of it.
○ I will sort it out, but not when you are shouting.
○ I am not sure that foul language is suitable for the classroom.
○ By using sexualized language you are making the situation worse.

These less provocative phrases could be repeated quietly with just a tinge of coldness. They are clear statements but don't demand immediate attention, and they place the emphasis on negotiation, not obedience.

Remember, pushing too hard in this phase can be catastrophic.

You have to be rock solid at times of crisis and not waver or deviate from the task of resolving the problem. Once you embark on managing crisis behaviour your expectations regarding the outcome must remain constant and consistent. Decide from the beginning of the challenge what you expect and clearly state what you want the outcome to be.

There must be no great deviation or massive changes of expectation. You must not say 'no' to behaviour and then allow it.

If you want a pupil to sit down, then eventually that must be achieved. You must not set a behaviour target and then accept anything less. If you say no swearing, then if the behaviour is to be resolved you must achieve clean speech.

You should not lower your expectations because that shows a crack, a weakness that will be played upon. Stand tall and be quietly confident in your attitude, but be consistent and predictable in your expectations.

STICK TO YOUR GUNS

When you are pushed hard by these pupils, you can often be forced into corners, and some responses can be close to ultimatums or threats. These ultimatums can be said in the heat of the moment and regretted for the rest of your teaching career.

The phrases used include:

o If you do that I will . . .
o Do that again and . . .
o Stop that or I will . . .
o Now you have done that I will have to . . .

These phrases can be changed into:

o It might be better not to do that because . . .
o It would be silly to do that again because it would make things worse . . .
o If you could stop doing that then perhaps we could . . .
o You know what happens when you do that. Would it not be better to perhaps . . .?

Taking away the threat or ultimatum leaves room for negotiation and prevents the pupil from feeling trapped. You are seen in a good light by the rest of the class and as a consequence they are far more likely to support you. Getting them on your side weighs heavily with the child in distress – he may sense things are going against him and may retreat.

Now if you get this tactic right at times of crisis it works really well, but you have to choose when to use it and have a pretty good idea that it's going to work.

There can be times in a challenging crisis when things narrow down to two or three quite distinct difficulties. These can include shouting abuse, swearing, pushing furniture, threatening, moving around the room, and making loud noises.

Select just one challenge from this array of behaviours and, ignoring the others, confront it quietly and repeatedly. Acknowledge the other behaviours but laser beam just one. Keep referring to it often, using the same words over and over again.

'Ok, I understand that but please just sit (pause). Yes I will deal with that as well but please just sit down (pause). That's fine, but please just sit down.'

Remain insistent and don't get angry. Give credit to other problems but keep to the task. If the famous, 'Are you going to make me?' comes up, just say, 'No, but I am asking you to please sit down. Now, could you sit please, and note that I am saying please and not shouting but asking.'

Keep calm, keep clear and stick to your guns because if you choose the right behaviour at the right time it does work.

Any movement towards challenging behaviour is best done in stages because the physical proximity to the challenge is to a degree dependent on the heat that closeness may cause. If our friend goes into crisis phase he is sensitive to threats and challengers.

GET CLOSER

o Acknowledge the behaviour by speech, facial expression or gesture.
o Move towards the pupil by working briefly with other pupils on the pathway to the trouble.
o Stop for a moment, test the air by communicating either by word or gesture, then stay back or move forward depending on the result.
o Wait for a while, then move forward slowly.
o Work towards getting as close as possible and, with confidence, communicate more directly.

Your closeness may cause a threat to a child in difficulty, but in the majority of cases he may actually be reassured by your presence. Your physical closeness also displays a lack of concern for whatever verbal aggression or physical threat he might be presenting.

When you reach your destination, be calm, careful and capable of meeting the challenge. If you can achieve that, you're on your way to success.

Once a crisis stage has begun it's extremely difficult to change the SEBD pupil's seating arrangements, as that in itself would become a major incident.

We can, however, make some changes regarding the pupils who sit around the troubles. If you're clever and quick thinking you can shift a few pupils when you see the trouble coming over the hill.

Try to surround our friend with reasonably positive pupils who are not likely to join in with whatever he might want to start. Use excuses for moving pupils around – regrouping, making special working groups, talking too much or not concentrating. Place them nearer the front board or further away depending on what kind of seating arrangement you think might lead to the difficult pupil being isolated.

Moving pupils around in a commanding but gentle manner can give you great credibility with the class and some respect from the difficult pupil.

At a less difficult time in the classroom try moving a few pupils around just to get the hang of it.

REARRANGE SEATING

PUT IT IN WRITING

When pupils reach this crisis stage their behaviour can, at times, be strange and bizarre. They often say and do things which are unusual, almost surreal. They seem to have a complete disregard for the consequences of what they say or do.

Move quietly towards your challenging pupil with paper and a pen and start to write down what is being said. Describe the behaviour out loud as you write it down. He will often react by asking you what you are doing.

Now you have an excellent opportunity to start a conversation about what is being said and what is being acted out but, most of all, the pupil will be concerned about the consequence of writing it all down.

By writing it down you are creating a record of what is happening and that in itself is a consequence. This can often have a significant effect on our friend's behaviour – he now knows there will be a record for everyone to see and that might prove difficult when all is quiet again.

Keeping a brief written record with time, date and place of all the difficult behaviour can be extremely useful.

The tactics in relation to crisis time are not necessarily to be carried out as single actions but should be combined to make effective interventions.

The difficult and dangerous period, if not resolved, will lead on to far more significant behaviour, therefore the combinations of different tactics will help you combat and hopefully quell a difficult challenge.

Pupils with different speeds of escalation and different patterns of behaviour will need different combinations of tactics to resolve the problem. You have to combine different ways of working with different pupils which not only match the behaviour you have to manage but also feel comfortable for you.

The tactic discussed should not be lifted off the peg but you should tailor it to suit your capabilities and personality. See what works; make a record, adapt and improve how you work at this difficult time.

Don't forget to congratulate yourself when things go well.

BRINGING ALL THE CRISIS TACTICS TOGETHER

Coping with profoundly difficult behaviours

IDEA

88

STRONG INTERVENTIONS

If behaviours have not been resolved at the crisis stage and the challenge becomes more profound, a different set of tactics should be considered.

Very angry pupils will probably have:

o increased blood pressure
o clenched teeth
o hunched shoulders
o a fast heartbeat
o tight and sweaty fists
o twitchy feet.

Wherever possible, check for these symptoms as they are a sign of how difficult the situation is. Be aware that at these times you can be in physical danger and your ability to physically move or prompt the child may be required. Only use physical prompting if you have been trained specifically for this work.

If the SEBD pupil's behaviour becomes physically dangerous, follow only agreed procedures. There should be a protocol in the school which gives an immediate response to physical danger.

The most crucial point of the call-out procedure is when to decide that behaviour is slipping away from your control and it is time to bring in support. Too early might exacerbate the problem, too late and the force required is that much greater and the destruction more significant.

If this problem occurs, ask yourself a few questions:

○ Does the pupil have a history of violence?
○ Have I felt anxious for my safety with this pupil before?
○ Has his behaviour followed similar patterns before and what was the outcome?
○ Could I have intervened earlier?
○ Did I do something to make the situation worse?
○ Are other pupils in the class getting excited by the violence?
○ Did I do things to the best of my ability and did it still become dangerous?

There are obviously many more questions you could ask; add them to the list and keep it available to scan if things get very difficult.

The decision to call out support is not a sign of your incompetence but more about the level of turbulence inside the challenging child.

STEADY EYE CONTACT

When more profound behaviour erupts it is essential that you appear calm and composed. This is a skill you must try to master. Although the behaviour may not be directed at you, it is your authority which is being flouted.

Eye contact can become crucial at this time and can project a sense of control and confidence. When communicating in any way with a distressed pupil it is important now to maintain full, uninterrupted eye contact.

You must maintain a strong, unblinking, calm gaze, with no narrowing, tightening and no expression, just clear, unconfused and steady.

If you have direct eye contact with the stressed child you must not look away but maintain a constant, unshakeable connection. This is about your strength of character confronting his wish to take control. At these crucial times by using strong eye contact you are showing your lack of fear and expressing your position as the authority in the room.

Without warning try this out on partners, relatives or close friends. Ask them how it felt, and work on the tactic. Try it on less troublesome pupils and see what their responses are like. Be aware that this is a very powerful tactic.

At these times a level of frustration can set in which the child cannot resolve. Previous triggers which could have contributed to the escalation now become more invasive and potentially more dangerous.

Without shouting, but with a strong voice and a good body posture, you must try to convey calmness and control.

TALKING

○ Be conscious of your breathing, taking slow, deep breaths which allow longer periods of speaking. Avoid running out of breath mid-sentence, as our friend will pick that up and read it as a sign of stress.

○ Talk slowly and calmly about the situation he has placed himself in, and be direct but not aggressive.

BODY POSTURE

○ Keep your body upright and check that your shoulders are relaxed – people have a tendency to lift their shoulders when threatened and this can be negatively rewarding for the disturbed pupil.

○ Don't clench your fists, but keep your hands loose and calm by your side.

○ Avoid stumbles or trips and be aware of any obstacles to movement.

○ If you start to sweat, take clothes off sooner rather than later. If possible, give a reason for taking clothes off otherwise this could appear to be a preparation for action – a surmise we don't need our pupil to make.

If you get these behaviours right it makes you feel more confident about your ability to deal with serious incidents and improves your performance.

It is important when a pupil is out of control that the behaviour is contained and other pupils are not hurt or property damaged, either of which could result in further escalation of the behaviour.

If you want to remove the class from the classroom you need to be proactive by sending notification of your intentions to the appropriate office. In most cases it is better to announce quietly to the class what you are doing and why. Emphasize how serious the situation is and explain what they have to do. Ask them quietly to pick up their bags and coats and just stand either outside the classroom or go to a previously agreed room or area. Ask them to leave in ones, twos, fives, whatever number you think would least disturb the heightened situation.

Tell the pupils leaving the classroom to walk slowly and ignore any comments, threats or abuse. Warn them not to make any remarks which might inflame the situation.

Throughout this process you must not forget our troubled pupil. Give him attention and try to continue a conversation. Don't allow him to think he is isolated, but suggest you are doing this because you would like the classroom to be quiet and free of distractions so you can really talk to him about his problem.

Once the class is cleared you can have a more private conversation and, in the absence of an audience, the pupil will often calm down.

There need to be at least two adults in the room – one for taking notes and listening and the other doing the talking. Always make sure that the door is open and the escape route for the pupil is clear.

When a pupil reaches a heightened anxiety state he feels isolated and peripheral to the class and can have a sense of rejection. This is not surprising as it is mostly true. All these feelings are adding to his arousal and need to be taken into account.

If you can get close to our friend it might be advisable to attempt light physical contact. This has to be done with caution and should, in most cases, be looked upon as a thermometer to test his temperature. The only safe areas at this stage are the upper and lower arm and the back of the hand; all other areas could be misunderstood.

If the reaction to any kind of touch is quite violent or rejecting then it's best not to try that again. If, however, the reaction to light physical contact is either none or it is perhaps accepted, then you have made considerable progress. However, don't continue, but wait for confirmation of acceptance which may come in the form of a less aggressive tone or a less aggressive statement of the perceived problem. Repeat the physical contact if the reconciliation appears to be starting.

Don't proceed to more invasive physical contact as this could be perceived as something other than comfort. At no time in this process should any hold or grip be placed on the pupil unless you have been trained in restraint and are confident about the methods you use.

NO CORNERING

One of the options if a pupil becomes too agitated would be for him to flee the classroom. Be very aware of that and make available an escape route for him.

If he can see no route out, a sense of being cornered might exacerbate the problem. A perception of being cornered can excite him and he could become violent.

o   If the classroom door is closed, open it. Don't say, 'Get out' (mistake), but perhaps point out that the door is open. He will know exactly what you mean and will then see it as an acceptable option.
o   Move objects out of the way that might prevent an escape.
o   Move pupils out of the way and even rearrange tables if necessary.

Make it clear if the pupil is out of control that to leave the room is acceptable. If there is a protocol in the school for this tactic then make sure the pupil is aware of where he might go and what to do.

The most important thing to remember when dealing with a pupil in a heightened sense of anxiety is that reason and most aspects of reality are not always applicable. Children in this state have little understanding of normal codes of behaviour and their motivations are almost entirely egocentric and self-indulgent.

This is not the time to engage in analysis, nor is it appropriate to encourage regression, although regressive behaviour is a feature of our friend's behaviour at this time.

As a teacher you might be able to put together some basic understanding of why the pupil has reached this point, but remember you see only the top of the iceberg – what lurks under the surface is unknown and often worse than you could imagine.

Sometimes the behaviour you have to work with will be outrageous, insulting and abusive. It can be very tempting, therefore, to start handing out future punishments – don't. This will simply inflame the situation and will give a negative target for our friend to aim at. Keep that in mind.

NO THERAPY

CRUCIAL FACTORS

The tactics recommended for dealing with extreme behaviour are complicated because you are dealing with chaotic, challenging and sometimes dangerous pupils with huge chunks of often paradoxical behaviour.

The factors you have to be aware of when working on the margins with these pupils are:

○ Do you have a strong enough will and desire to win over the most difficult and demanding pupils?
○ Do you have sufficient knowledge and experience of working with pupils at this hard end of the market?
○ Do you need training in the management of these extreme behaviours?
○ Is the quality of the call-out, back-up support you receive from the school adequate?
○ Are the extremes of behaviour you are expected to work with containable?
○ Is the general level of discipline in the school good enough to support a calm classroom?
○ Is the quality of support services in the school, including SMT, SENCO and important external services, adequate?
○ And, perhaps most important of all, do you have any empathy for these challenging children?

Your ability to be an effective teacher and cope with challenging pupils included in your class is also dependent on the ability of the school to support you appropriately. Work hard, be diligent and keep clear, up-to-date records of all incidents, including the school's participation in major challenges.

Recovery phase

The one thing I can say for certain is that our SEBDs do eventually calm down. However, this is by no means the end of the job because in the recovery phase they are very vulnerable to many triggers. If not carefully handled they can flare up again quite quickly.

Remove the pupil to a quiet room as quickly as possible; make sure it is away from the classroom. Begin the conversation about what has just occurred, sticking initially to the simple facts. Write out the incident with the pupil, showing just how important it is to understand what happened. If possible, this is best done by the class teacher who weathered the storm and has some sort of relationship with the now often quite depressed pupil. Take it very steady, don't rush, and try very hard to prevent agitation and stress.

Don't talk too much. Let the pupil do as much of that as possible, and guide the conversation rather than lead it. Suggest shouting is not appropriate, but straight talking is very healthy.

If the pupil is still outraged at some injustice, say you will deal with it but only in a quiet and non-aggressive way. Do not collude, but at the same time don't challenge nonsense, let it pass as there will be time for all that later. Our friend knows he's talking rubbish but he might still be in defensive mode. Give him time to settle.

As recovery continues so the pupil should start to settle, a joke might be cracked, a cup of tea/water/squash downed and stretching, sometimes yawning, might occur. Try to hold a normal conversation, perhaps about football, a soap opera you both watch, or a special TV show. Let the mood settle and then return to the troubles, gradually fitting the whole picture together, listing perhaps chronologically what happened and who were the main participants.

Make clear notes which the pupil can agree with. Try to keep it light, returning to patches of normal conversation in between.

If all goes well with the recovery phase, the pupil might apologize. This is obviously a good thing for him to do, but you should not demand it. Patience is required as it may take time for our friend to reduce the stress he has experienced.

There may also be guilt feelings, either about what has been said or harm and damage caused to property and/or people. This is more difficult to deal with as the damage could be considerable.

You can't step back from this one and you must not condone the damage done, but you don't have to raise your voice and you must not be aggressive. The guilt and the apology must be dealt with carefully because if the matter can be concluded appropriately then the likelihood of a recurrence is reduced.

Try to finish on a positive note.

DEALING WITH GUILT AND APOLOGIES

REPARATION

When you are confident that the anger and stress have reduced sufficiently for discussions to take place regarding damage then you could start talking about repair and reparation.

It must depend on the severity of the damage and abuse, but carefully managed this can often be a turning point with more sensitive pupils. Although they may not appear sensitive, they are often affected quite significantly by damage they might have caused.

There are several ways you can manage this, for example by suggesting that the pupil might:

o help put the classroom back together
o repair with your help any furniture which may have been damaged
o stick or glue back together any damaged books or displays
o help a fellow pupil who might have been hurt or frightened by the incident
o make apologies to any other adult or pupil who might have found the incident distressing.

Most of this reparation should be done in private, away from the gaze of children who might find the repair or apology amusing or, worse, a reason to restart the problem all over again.

If done well reparation is probably the best way of preventing major incidents in the future.

To be effective and happy in your work with these SEBD pupils you have to look for a balance between you as a person, with all your flaws and idiosyncrasies, and the person you have to construct to get the management of these difficult pupils right.

There has to be a bit of a 'false you' which you attach when you enter school; a role you have to play. This is not dishonest, but being a professional. Try to:

○ balance what you are happy with and what is possible within the bounds of your personality
○ search for a way of behaving which controls the whole class and allows you to teach, because that's what you get paid for
○ think creatively about the job of teaching. If you do this there is every chance that you will evolve into a confident and stylish professional. If you don't think creatively you will start to blame the pupils, and that is a road to ruin.

SEBD pupils are the most difficult and challenging of all special needs children for a teacher to manage – get it right and the satisfaction of doing a good job is almost overwhelming. Best of luck.

FINDING THE BALANCE